WHO WAS
TUTANKHAMUN?

DAVID NASMYTH

ILLUSTRATED BY MIKE WHITE

First published in Great Britain 1998 by
Macdonald Young Books, an imprint of
Wayland Books Ltd
61 Western Road
Hove
East Sussex BN3 1JD

Find Macdonald Young Books on the Internet
at: http://www.myb.co.uk

Series concept and text
© Wendy and Sally Knowles

Design and illustrations
© Macdonald Young Books

Edited by Wendy Knowles
Designed by Celia Hart
Series design by David Fordham
Map artist: Brett Breckon

Printed and bound in Portugal by Edições ASA

ISBN: 0 7500 2377 5

The front cover portrait of Tutankhamun
is based on the gold mummy mask of him
found in the tomb.

Dates
The dates of the Egyptian dynasties and the
pharaohs who ruled them are still the subject
of discussion. The dates used in this book are
accurate, within about 20 years.

Photograph acknowledgements:

We are grateful to the following for permission
to reproduce photographs:
Front cover: Robert Harding Picture Library/
F.L. Kenett Collection.

The Ancient Egypt Picture Library, pages 13,
16(t), 18(c) (watercolour copy by Nina de Garis
Davies), 41, (Egyptian Museum, Cairo) 24,
30 (b), 31(t) and 35(b); Ancient Art &
Architecture Collection, pages 9 (t) (R Bell),
15(c) and 25 (b) (Mary Jelliffe); The Earl of
Carnarvon, Highclere Castle, page 10 (t); C M
Dixon/The Louvre, Paris, page 18(b); Gift of
Edward W Forbes, courtesy, Museum of Fine
Arts, Boston, page 25 (t); Werner Forman
Archive, pages 15(t), 15(b), 21(l), 40(b), (The
British Museum, London) 18(t), 33(t) and
33(b), (Detroit Institute of Art) 35(tl),
(Egyptian Museum, Berlin)17(r), (Egyptian
Museum, Cairo) 16(b) and 31(b), (Dr E
Strouhal) 33(c), 38 and 39(b); The Griffith
Institute, Ashmolean Museum, Oxford, pages
10(bl), 11(t), 12(t), 26(l); Robert Harding
Picture Library/F L Kenett Collection, pages
8(t), 9(c), 9(b), 10(br), 12(b), 17(l), 20, 21(br),
22, 23, 26(br), 27, 28, 29, 30(t), 32, 36, 39(t),
40(t); James Morris/Axiom Photographic
Agency/Luxor Museum, Egypt, page 37;
Rijksmuseum van Oudheden, Leiden, NL,
page 35(tr).

Picture Research by Valerie Mulcahy

CONTENTS

TUTANKHAMUN'S EGYPT

Following a brief reign of 9 years, the young boy-king of Egypt, Tutankhamun, was laid to rest in a rock-cut tomb close to his forefathers, in about 1325 BC. Since its discovery in 1922, 33 centuries later, his tomb with its gold treasures has excited people's imagination. It remains one of the world's most exciting archaeological discoveries.

One of the richest jewels found in Tutankhamun's tomb. The centre is a scarab beetle, a symbol of resurrection.

WHAT WAS TUTANKHAMUN'S EGYPT LIKE?

Tutankhamun lived and died during a period of ancient Egyptian history known to historians as the New Kingdom. This period came to an end just before 1000 BC. Historians divide Egyptian history into 32 families or dynasties, which are periods when whole families ruled over the country. Tutankhamun was part of the 18th Dynasty.

Tutankhamun was not an important king. He never emerged as a ruler in his own right, and his tomb was not particularly rich. However, his tomb has survived and the tombs of other kings have not.

This portrait of Tutankhamun is based upon the gold mummy mask of him found in his tomb. He is wearing the royal diadem (crown), adorned with the head of the vulture-goddess, Nekhabet, and a cobra.

WHERE WAS HIS TOMB?

The Valley of the Kings, on the west bank of the Nile near Luxor in Egypt, is one of the most desolate spots on earth. This is why the ancient Egyptians chose it to be the burial place of their kings, who were known in the New Kingdom as pharaohs. One by one the pharaohs of Egypt died, and were buried here, along with all their treasures.

The Valley of the Kings. Nearly all the pharaohs and some queens of the New Kingdom were buried in this remote desert valley in Western Thebes.

The finest of the pendants in the treasure found on Tutankhamun represents the fierce vulture-goddess Nekhabet. She protected the dead king against danger.

The Egyptians thought of their kings as living gods. They believed that when a king died, his soul, or 'ka' would leave his body and then fly to heaven. Here it would join his father, the sun god, Ra, and journey across heaven every day, watching over Egypt.

WHAT HAPPENED WHEN A KING DIED?

The king's body had to be preserved because if it wasn't, there was no possibility of an after-life. His name had to be recorded on his tomb and the tomb provided with all that he needed for the long journey into the next life. We call these preserved bodies 'mummies'. The mummies of the dead kings were surrounded with all the treasures that they had used and needed during their earthly lives. The ordinary ancient Egyptians knew this. By 1000 BC all known royal tombs in the Valley of the Kings had been robbed of their treasures.

One of the 4 small gold 'mummy' coffins holding the king's internal organs. They were found inside an alabaster (semi-transparent stone) chest.

THE MISSING KING AND HIS TREASURE

One man thought the treasure had not all been looted. He was an Englishman named Howard Carter, and he knew the tombs in the Valley of the Kings very well. The pharaohs' tombs were all there, except one: the tomb of a king who ruled Egypt between about 1336 and 1325 BC. His name was Tutankhamun. Carter had no money, but he persuaded a rich man named Lord Carnarvon to pay for his work in the Valley. Year after year they dug there, but found nothing. Finally in 1921, Carnarvon told Carter that he would give him money for just one more year. This was his last chance.

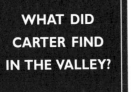

WHAT DID CARTER FIND IN THE VALLEY?

4th November 1922 started out as an ordinary day for Carter. But then one of his workmen noticed something on the rocky floor of the Valley where they were working. He cleared away the sand, found a step, and, below the step, another step. Soon they had 16 steps, leading down to an ancient door, cut into the rock. There, on the door, was the name of the king who had been buried inside. It was Tutankhamun. There was a small hole in the corner of the door, probably made by ancient robbers. It had been sealed over with plaster.

Howard Carter believed that Tutankhamun's tomb still awaited discovery and might even be intact. His perseverance was finally rewarded on 26 November 1922.

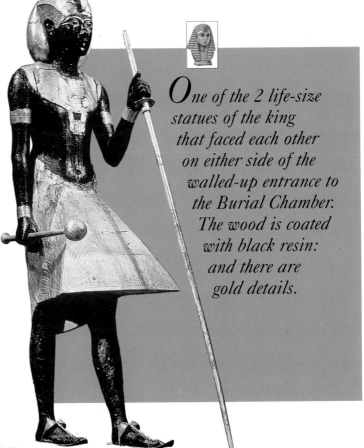

Lord Carnavon first went to Egypt for its warm climate because he was ill. There, he became interested in Egyptology and provided the money for Howard Carter's search for the tomb of Tutankhamun.

One of the 2 life-size statues of the king that faced each other on either side of the walled-up entrance to the Burial Chamber. The wood is coated with black resin: and there are gold details.

WHAT LAY BEHIND THE DOOR OF THE TOMB?

Behind the door was a corridor, running into the rock. It was blocked with stones and rubble. Here too the ancient robbers had been, leaving a small tunnel. But at the end of the corridor the excavators found a second door, blocked with plaster. On 26 November 1922, Carter made a hole in this second door, and lit a match to test for poisonous gases coming out of the rock. Everything was safe. He shone a torch through the hole, and then he fell silent.

Howard Carter peers into the hole in the tomb door. Carnarvon recalled afterwards. 'He did not say anything for 2 or 3 minutes, but kept me in rather painful suspense. I thought I had been disappointed again, and I said, "Can you see anything?" "Yes, yes," he replied, "wonderful things." '

A photo taken by the excavators of their first sight of the Antechamber of the tomb with all its shimmering golden treasure.

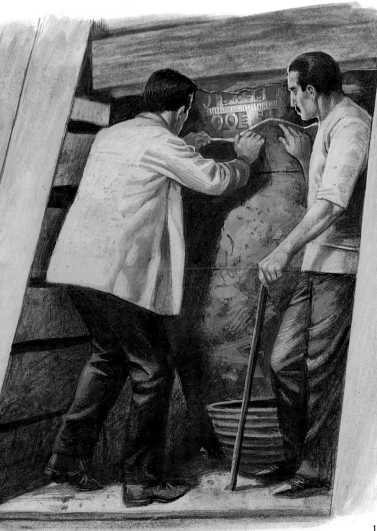

As Carter's eyes got used to the darkness, he saw one treasure after another: boxes, jewels, three large couches or beds with the heads of strange animals on them, statues, jars of food and wine and model boats. And everywhere he looked, he saw the gleam of gold.

WHERE WAS THE KING?

To the left, Carter saw two life-size statues of the king, standing in the dark. They were facing each other, and holding long golden staffs as if they were guarding something. Between them he could make out something else. It was another door. This time there was no hole in it. The robbers had not got beyond it. Everything behind it would be exactly as it had been left, at the time of the king's funeral.

THE TOMB

Carter called the room he had discovered the Antechamber. Here it was clear that the robbers had penetrated, probably not long after the funeral of the king. But it was also clear that the tomb guards had caught them. The guards had tidied up the room in a hurry, and then repaired the doors. They left Tutankhamun's tomb. Years later another king built his own tomb next to it. The stones and rubble from the tunnelling of this tomb were piled up, over the small door to Tutankhamun's tomb. This is what had saved Tutankhamun's treasures.

One robber had found a box of gold rings, which he took and threaded on to a handkerchief. This handkerchief, photographed by the excavators, was still on the floor, where the thief had dropped it as he tried to escape from the tomb guards.

WHAT WAS BEHIND THE DOOR?

When Carter and Carnarvon broke through the door between the 2 statues what they saw puzzled them. It looked just like another wall, but a wall made of gold and precious blue stones. They found that they could just squeeze in front of this wall, and follow it round, making sure not to tread on the treasures which were piled up on the floor. At last they realised that they were looking at the outside of a huge gold shrine. It was covered with religious symbols written in the sacred writing of the Egyptians, known as hieroglyphs. Inside this shrine, there turned out to be another shrine, making 4 in all.

There was a little room to the side of the gold shrine containing some of the finest treasures. Its entrance was guarded by this large wooden image of the black jackal-god Anubis, god of cemeteries.

WHAT WAS INSIDE THE LAST SHRINE?

There was a magnificent stone container, known as a sarcophagus, covered with a lid, which was so heavy that it needed a modern crane to lift it. Inside this there was a coffin of gilded wood, made to resemble the body of the dead king. Within this was a second coffin, even more richly decorated. And inside this was a third coffin, the finest of all, made entirely of gold. The gold of this coffin would be worth several millions of pounds today.

The nest of 3 gold coffins containing the mummified body of the dead king is placed inside the sarcophagus (stone coffin).

Tutankhamun's solid gold funeral mask. As the experts looked at the face beneath the mask, they recognised that the portrait on the gold mask looked just like him.

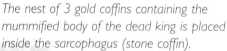

WHERE WAS THE KING?

Finally, there was the body of the king, carefully wrapped in linen and covered with elaborate jewels to decorate him in the next world. Over his face was a mask, made of gold and a precious blue stone called lapis lazuli. He was not more than 18 or 19 years old.

The shrines had been carefully made in pieces, which could be reconstructed inside the tomb. At one end were huge doors, of wood covered in gold, and secured with ropes and wax seals.

BEGINNINGS

Historians think that Tutankhamun was born in about 1345 BC. This was a period of great conflict and change in ancient Egyptian history. It was an age of international power-politics, religious turmoil and artistic creativity, largely brought about by a revolutionary king called Akhenaten who was probably Tutankhamun's father. If so, he had a very unusual man for a father.

WHAT WAS UNUSUAL ABOUT AKHENATEN?

In about 1350 BC Akhenaten decided that all the hundreds of gods which the Egyptians worshipped were false. Instead, there was only one god, whom Akhenaten thought was present in the disc or globe of the sun. This god was called the Aten, meaning 'the Disc'. The Aten, he decided, would be the new god of Egypt, and all the old temples would be closed down. When Tutankhamun was born he was in fact given the name Tut-ankh-Aten, which means 'Living Image of the Sun Disc'.

Unlike the traditional closed temples of the old gods, Akhenaten's temple for the Aten was left open to the sky. His decision to replace the old gods and in particular Amun, the old chief god, with the Aten was not popular with most Egyptians.

Akhenaten, accompanied by his queen, Nefertiti, makes an offering to the god of the sun disc, the Aten.

Traditional religious practices and festivals underpinned the whole structure of Egyptian society. They were part of most Egyptians' everyday lives. Akhenaten's decision to attack all the old gods, and close down their temples affected everyone. But it was his decision to attack the god, Amun, who looked after both Egypt and the king, that caused the greatest stir.

The great temple of Amun at Karnak, Thebes, the centre of the cult of Amun. Massive stone gateways guarded the entrance. Behind them was a series of courts and colonnades leading to a dark inner sanctuary.

Horus, the falcon-god and sky-god. The pharaoh was his representative on earth.

HOW DID HIS CLOSURE OF THE TEMPLES AFFECT EGYPT?

The temples in ancient Egypt were not like sacred buildings today. They had an important part to play in the smooth running of the country. The Chief Priest of Amun might easily have previously been a senior court official or a general. His responsibilities would have included overseeing the craftsmen working on the royal tombs, and public works in general.

The sacred boat carrying Amun's statue. During the joyful festival of Opet, which took place each year at the time of the Nile floods, the statue of Amun at Karnak was taken from its sanctuary and transported down the river so that all could see it.

TUTANKHAMUN'S FAMILY

Akhenaten was married to one of the most beautiful women in history. She was called Nefertiti. A limestone bust of her survives and is now in a museum in Berlin, in Germany. But Akhenaten also had another wife, called Kiya. Historians suspect that she was Tutankhamun's mother. Kiya died when Tutankhamun was very young, and he was brought up by Nefertiti.

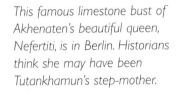

This famous limestone bust of Akhenaten's beautiful queen, Nefertiti, is in Berlin. Historians think she may have been Tutankhamun's step-mother.

DID HE HAVE ANY BROTHERS AND SISTERS?

He had an older brother called Smenkhkare. When Akhenaten died in about 1336 BC, this brother succeeded him as king, but he died after only a year. Some objects belonging to him were found in the tomb. Tutankhamun also had 6 half-sisters, who were the daughters of Nefertiti and Akhenaten.

Scenes from the life of King Akhenaten's family show them as a happy and loving family. Unlike previous kings of Egypt the royal family are shown as an ordinary family.

A limestone relief of Nefertiti with her 2 youngest daughters. The oldest daughter, Meritaten, wearing her hair in a side-lock, is being given an earring by her father.

WHO WERE TUTANKHAMUN'S GRANDPARENTS?

His grandfather was Amenhotep III, a very great pharaoh, and his grandmother was called Tiye. Tutankhamun probably had happy memories of her. In his tomb was found a tiny container, and inside this was a lock of a woman's hair. A label said that this hair belonged to Queen Tiye, who had been Akhenaten's mother.

When her husband grew old, she took on his duties. This was unusual, most Egyptian queens carried out no official duties.

An ebony head of Queen Tiye. This is kept in the Berlin Museum. After Tiye's husband, Amenhotep III, died, princes from foreign lands wrote to her to persuade her to use her influence with her son, Akhenaten.

A tiny gold statuette found with the small 'mummy' coffin. It contained a lock of Queen Tiye's hair.

Tutankhamun and his sisters visit a new temple site with Akhenaten. The effect of Akhenaten's changes to the country's religion was enormous.

TUTANKHAMUN'S CHILDHOOD

A small, painted 18th-dynasty glass vase in the form of a fish, found at Amarna.

Tutankhamun's family lived in the newly built city of Akhetaten, in the middle of Egypt, which nowadays we call Amarna. This new city of Amarna had been founded by Akhenaten to be the great centre for his new religion of Aten and may well have been the birth-place of Tutankhamun. Here in Amarna, Akhenaten encouraged artists to develop new styles of painting and sculpture.

WHAT WAS DIFFERENT ABOUT AMARNA?

It was unlike most other Egyptian cities of this time with their houses crowded together along narrow, twisting alleys. Akhenaten designed his new city of Amarna with wide streets and spacious, one-storeyed villas each surrounded by a garden. In the ceremonial centre of the city, a bridge over the main avenue linked the residential part of the palace with the grander, more public palace, designed for the king's official duties. However, Tutankhamun probably spent his early years in another beautiful palace. This palace, known as the North Palace, was set well apart from the rest of the city.

The walls of the hall called the Green Room in the North Palace were decorated with the most beautiful paintings of kingfishers, flowers and animals.

A beautiful glazed tile from Amarna.

WHAT WAS THE NORTH PALACE LIKE?

It was a spacious house, with a pool full of fish, and a big garden shaded by trees. In the middle was a large hall with stone columns. It was used for entertaining in the shade, away from the hot sun. There was also a hall historians call the 'Green Room', with great windows looking out on to the gardens.

WHY DO WE BELIEVE HE LIVED THERE?

When archaeologists excavated the palace they found the private rooms of the king and his wife. Across a small courtyard were the bedrooms of the 6 little princesses, Tutankhamun's half-sisters. They also found a larger room which they think might have been used as a playroom. Its walls were streaked with paint as if children had wiped their paintbrushes there. Beneath the rubble of the palace they found brushes and paint-boxes.

The palace that Tutankhamun grew up in would have had bathrooms leading off the bedrooms. The floors were waterproof, made of a stone slab, with a slightly raised border. Waste water drained off into a hole in the floor or else through a drain into the street. There was no piped water.

Tutankhamun and his sisters play together at the palace in Akhetaten (Amarna).

TUTANKHAMUN AT SCHOOL

Children began their education very early in Egypt. Tutankhamun probably began learning to read at the age of four. Once he could read and do simple arithmetic, then he would have had to learn how to write the ancient Egyptian language. One of the most interesting objects found in Tutankhamun's tomb is also one of the smallest. It is his writing kit.

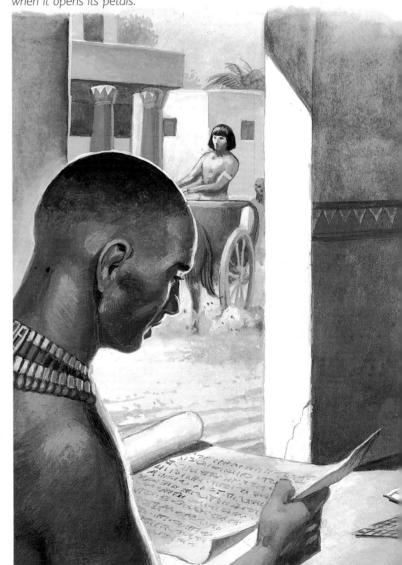

This head of Tutankhamun was found at the entrance of the tomb. It portrays the king as a young child emerging from a lotus flower when it opens its petals.

WHAT IS HIS WRITING KIT LIKE?

It is an oblong piece of ivory just under 30cm (12 inches) long, with a pocket in the centre to hold his set of reed pens. There are small cakes of red and black ink set into this; all he had to do was to dip a new pen into water, and moisten the ink, just as you do with a paint-box today. The inscription on the pen-holder says that it was given to the young king by his half-sister, the princess Meritaten. Perhaps this means that she had learnt to write, as girls in ancient Egypt sometimes did.

ANCIENT EGYPTIAN WRITING
The ancient Egyptians wrote rather like we do, with a pen on paper, except that Egyptian pens were made out of long reeds which grew by the river. The ends of these reeds were hammered out, until they became rather like a modern brush. Writing was very like painting.

*A*NCIENT *E*GYPTIAN *P*APER
*O*rdinary schoolchildren would have
used wooden boards. Tutankhamun was
lucky enough to use a very expensive paper.
It was made out of reeds cut from
a plant called papyrus which grew
near the waters of the Nile.

WHERE DID HE GO TO SCHOOL?

He may have gone
to a school in one
of the temples, but
more likely a teacher
came to him in the
palace and gave him
lessons on his own.
He probably wasn't all that keen on school.
Many of the other objects in his tomb show
that his main interests were playing outdoor
games, and racing around in his chariot
hunting animals. Perhaps he found school dull.

An 18th-dynasty wall painting
of a hippo in a papyrus
thicket. To make papyrus
paper the Egyptians flattened
out the stalks of the papyrus
and laid them in rows. They
then covered them with a
second layer of stalks running
at right angles to the first.
The whole lot was then
pressed heavily upon until it
dried out and became like
a sheet of paper.

WAS HE A GOOD STUDENT?

We do not know if
he was a good
student. But with his
pen set was found an
eraser, made of ivory
with a gold handle. It is
wedge-shaped, with a
long sharp edge at the top. This was used for
rubbing out mistakes from the surface of the
papyrus paper. When this was done, the eraser
could be turned round, and the curved knob
at the end used to polish over the area so
that something else could be written in
the space.

Tutankhamun with his teacher. Judging by the other
objects in his tomb, he was not keen on school work.

Tutankhamun's ivory
writing kit (far right) and
his case for writing reeds.

ACCESSION TO THE THRONE

On the death of his brother, Smenkhkare, Tutankhamun became king. He was about 9 years old. As the son of the sun-god, Ra, the mythical first king of Egypt, the king was thought to control the weather. Every morning Tutankhamun would have carried out a ceremony in the temple which was repeated by priests in every temple. As a living god the pharaoh wore a bull's tail, a symbol of strength and fertility. Now that he was king, Tutankhamun was supposed to be married. This was so that he could pass on the god's blood to his children.

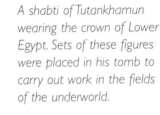

A shabti of Tutankhamun wearing the crown of Lower Egypt. Sets of these figures were placed in his tomb to carry out work in the fields of the underworld.

Tutankhamun is crowned king of Egypt. He holds a crook and a flail. These were symbols of the king's authority.

WHOM DID HE MARRY?

His half-sister, Ankhesenamun. She was the third of Akhenaten and Nefertiti's 6 daughters and older than him. She and Tutankhamun would have played together in the palace of Amarna. They might even have been childhood sweethearts, as they must have been told early on that they were to marry.

A head of Tutankhamun's queen, Ankhesenamun. This is taken from a scene on the back of the gold-plated throne. She is wearing a wig with 2 plumes, a sign that she is a goddess.

In the tomb there was a strange wooden box containing locks of hair belonging to the couple. The hair was probably cut off at the time of their wedding and put into the box to mix together, signifying that they were married.

WHY DID HE MARRY HER?

She was more royal than he was. The eldest son and daughter of the king and queen were the royal heir and heiress. Because the god's blood ran in the pharaoh's veins, the heir and heiress would often marry each other to keep it undiluted. Ordinary Egyptians were free to marry who they liked, but for kings it was different. As the 'wife of god' Ankhesenamun's position was very special, but she would have had no official duties.

Tutankhamun and Ankhesenamun depicted on the gold-plated shrine. She wears a dress of pleated linen and is shown affectionately fastening a double necklace round his neck. He is wearing a short wig with little curls.

DID TUTANKHAMUN LOVE HIS WIFE?

Yes, judging from the scenes in his tomb. On the lid of one of the chests found in his tomb there is a scene of the two of them when they were still very young. The king is leaning on a staff while the queen offers him mandrake fruits, which were a symbol of passion. In another scene on the back of the king's throne, she is shown affectionately anointing his collar.

RETURN TO THE OLD CAPITAL, AND THE OLD GODS

The new religion of Akhenaten had been very unpopular in Egypt, especially with the priests, because it meant closing down the temples. The Egypt that Tutankhamun inherited was a country on the point of collapse, threatened by religious quarrels and by enemies abroad. One of the young king's first acts was to reject the new religion of Akhenaten and move the court back to Thebes.

A statue of Tutankhamun as the moon-god, Khons, son of Amun. It was found in the temple of Amun at Karnak.

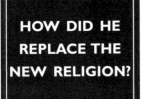

HOW DID HE REPLACE THE NEW RELIGION?

He replaced the Aten with Amun, the old chief god, and brought back all the old gods. So Tutankhaten, as he was, changed his name to Tut-ankh-Amun, 'Living Image of Amun', which is what we call him. The administrative capital of Egypt was moved back from Amarna to Memphis, with Thebes, the home of the god Amun, as the religious centre of the country. The change proved to be very popular, and the temple of Amun grew richer and richer.

Tutankhamun, wearing the crown of Upper and Lower Egypt, honours the old chief god, Amun. Within a year of his accession to the throne Tutankhamun had officially restored the cult of Amun. Behind him is his adviser Ay, the Chief Priest of Amun.

WAS TUTANKHAMUN REALLY IN CHARGE?

It's unlikely. He was still too young at this stage to take an active part in government. The chief priest of Amun was an elderly man called Ay. It was Ay who probably had the idea of changing the religion and persuaded the young king to go along with it. Ay was related to Tutankhamun's step-mother, Nefertiti. He was really the power behind the scenes in Egypt throughout Tutankhamun's reign.

Tutankhamun's advisor, Ay, depicted as the God Nile. He became king on the death of Tutankhamun.

Ay was only able to rule Egypt on Tutankhamun's behalf with the approval of the army. This was commanded by a general named Horemheb. He was the other most powerful man in Egypt apart from Ay.

WHY WAS AY KEEN TO BRING BACK THE OLD RELIGION ?

Since he was Chief Priest, he would benefit greatly if the old temples were re-opened. Also, he wanted to secure Tutankhamun's position as king and to avoid a religious war between the supporters of the old religion and the supporters of the new religion. The army general, Horemheb did not want the army to get involved in a civil war. It suited him to support Ay for the time being. But these very powerful men both wanted to be king, and hated each other.

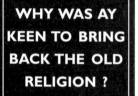

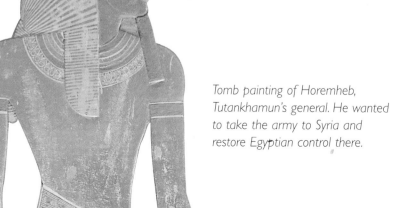

Tomb painting of Horemheb, Tutankhamun's general. He wanted to take the army to Syria and restore Egyptian control there.

STILL ONLY A CHILD

For most of his reign Tutankhamun was still only a child. In his tomb there were a number of his favourite toys and cherished possessions which he had not wanted to part with. Perhaps he was saving them for his own children one day. There was even a royal 'toy chest'.

The excavators' photo of Tutankhamun's 'toy chest'. When found it contained a mix of objects: jewellery, a board game, a pair of slings, and the king's fire-making equipment.

WHAT WAS INSIDE HIS 'TOY CHEST' ?

This contained a mix of favourite objects – jewellery, a game-board, a pair of slings, and the king's fire-making equipment. He probably spent many happy hours sitting in the palace garden playing the serpent game with his friends – a game rather similar to our snakes and ladders – or making the sparks fly from his wooden lighter.

WERE THERE ANY UNUSUAL OBJECTS?

One of the most interesting objects in the king's tomb is a dagger with an iron blade. This was very unusual in Tutankhamun's day. The handle is also strange, since it is decorated with gold spirals. This design was not Egyptian at all, but Syrian. Syria was under Egyptian control at the time, and young princes were often sent from there to go to school in Egypt. The dagger was probably a present to Tutankhamun from one of the Syrian boys who went to classes with him, or it might even have been swapped.

The king's two daggers, one with a blade of gold and the other with a blade of iron. The blade of the iron dagger was still clean and shining at the time of its discovery.

26

In the tomb was a long, plain reed stick which stood out from the other elaborately decorated items in the tomb. On it there was a simple inscription that says that he cut it himself, probably one day when he was playing by the banks of the Nile. He was obviously allowed some freedom. There was also his vast collection of walking sticks, his model boats and a small chair with an inlaid wooden back. He must have used this when he was a boy, perhaps at meal times or when he was learning his sums.

The young Tutankhamun receives an iron dagger from a Syrian prince. Syria was under Egyptian control at this time, and young princes were often sent from there to go to school in Egypt.

The tomb contained a number of model wooden boats. Some of these wooden boats would have been made as funerary models, specially to go in the tomb, but some of them must have been his own model toy boats. His finger-print was found on one, so he must have played with it one day when his hands were dirty.

THE BOY BEHIND THE MASK – AT 12

When the archaeologists finally unwrapped the mummy cases surrounding Tutankhamun's body, they found the body of a slightly built teenager about 1.65m (5ft 5in) tall. Studies of his teeth enabled them to work out his age as being about 18 or 19.

WHAT DID HE LOOK LIKE?

We have a good idea what Tutankhamun looked like, both as a small child and as a young boy and teenager. There is a small head of him, made of painted wood, which shows him coming out of a lotus flower. The Egyptians believed the sun-god did this at the beginning of the world. Tutankhamun must have been about 5 when this was made. When he was 12, he posed for a wooden model of himself, a dummy, which tailors could use to fit his clothes properly. Both these models were found in his tomb.

Tutankhamun posed for this wooden model of himself at about 12, so that tailors could use it as a dummy to fit his clothes. The ears are pierced to hold earrings.

The young king loved to go hunting in his chariot in the marshes around the Nile. Several chariots were found in the tomb.

DID HE HAVE A FAVOURITE HOBBY ?

Yes. He loved hunting. On a magnificently painted box from his tomb, Tutankhamun is shown in his two-wheeled chariot, hunting a whole pride of lions with his bow and arrows. He also loved hunting ostriches. In the tomb were found two great fans, made out of gold and ostrich feathers. An inscription on one of them says that the feathers were taken from birds which he had caught himself.

When the ostrich fans were found, the feathers were still perfect, because the air in the tomb had not changed for over 3,000 years. But within minutes of being discovered, the feathers crumbled to dust.

The king's fly-whisk made of wood covered with gold. The curved edge is pierced with holes into which white and dark brown ostrich feathers were originally fixed. The king is depicted alone on his chariot hunting a pair of ostriches in the desert with his hound.

CLOTHES AND TRAPPINGS OF A KING

Just like anyone who has packed for a long journey, Tutankhamun's tomb was full of the clothes and preparations necessary for maintaining his appearance. Some of them were things that he must actually have worn and some of them were things that the Egyptians believed their king would need in the next world.

WHAT CLOTHES DID HE WEAR?

On the painted ivory panel of a wooden chest he is shown wearing a short, pleated kilt with 2 ends crossed over and tucked in at the hips, under a belt that is tied into a bow. This was the standard male clothing for Egypt for thousands of years. Most of the clothes found in the tomb were made of linen, the most common material for garments at this time. Some clothes were very elaborate, decorated with jewellery and gold sequins or exquisite beadwork. He had tunics and belts, robes for state occasions, and sandals and gloves. There was even a pair of small mittens which he must have had when very young.

This portrait of Tutankhamun is taken from a panel of the painted ivory chest. Most of the clothes found in his tomb were made of linen.

Inside the king's tomb the archaeologists even found his underwear – triangular, finely pleated linen loincloths. The only things missing in the tomb were his royal crowns.

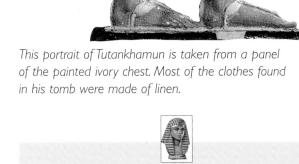

One of the archaeologists excavating the tomb wrote to his wife, 'I made a strange find among the king's robes today – a child's glove of cloth, belonging to a child I should say three or four years old. I imagine it must have been one of his own.'

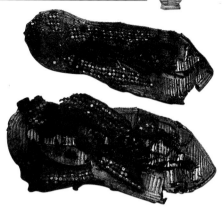

WHAT WERE HIS SHOES LIKE?

Carter recorded 93 items or fragments of footwear in the tomb. The types of shoes ranged from simple basketwork sandals, of which there were 32 pairs, to sandals of leather sumptuously patterned with beadwork or gold. He had sandals with figures of foreign peoples on their soles, so that he could walk on them, and so conquer them as if by magic.

Elaborate sandals sumptuously patterned with gold and beadwork. Just one of the many pairs of sandals found.

The young king sitting upon the so-called 'golden throne'. He is wearing jointed gold armour, the crown of Upper and Lower Egypt and a gold collar set with coloured glass.

WERE THERE ANY JEWELS IN THE TOMB?

According to the lists found in the tomb detailing the contents of the jewellery boxes, a lot of the more precious pieces had been taken by the tomb robbers. However there were still many items of jewellery left, made of gold and precious stones and sometimes glass, which was a rarity at that time. Some of the jewels would have been worn by him during his life; others, with religious scenes, were made specially for the tomb.

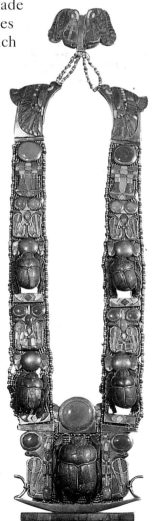

A scarab necklace. Here, the scarab (sun-god) pushes a dung-ball representing the sun. Together they represent sunrise and rebirth. The scarab is carried in a sacred boat. It was placed upon the mummy to ensure that the king would live again.

LEISURE AND PLEASURE

The objects in the tomb tell us something about the private life of Tutankhamun and his queen. Their palace was elegantly furnished, the furniture carved with animal heads and inlaid with ivory, ebony or glass. Elaborate banquets would have been an important part of their lives as they would have been for most wealthy Egyptians.

Tutankhamun and his queen at a banquet. Like most ancient Egyptians, the king and his wife probably enjoyed listening to popular music. Music would have been an essential part of any feast. Egyptians believed that it made the gods happy.

An ebony and ivory gaming set. There were 4 games of senet found in the tomb. Players had to get their counters to the middle of the board. You could land on good and bad luck squares along the way.

*B*read was the staple food of rich and poor alike. Most people lived on a diet of mainly vegetables, fruit and fish. Meat could only be afforded by wealthy ancient Egyptians.

An 18th-dynasty wall painting showing elegantly dressed guests seated on chairs and stools being served wine by servants.

WHAT DID THE KING AND QUEEN EAT AND DRINK?

In one scene on the golden shrine, the queen pours wine for Tutankhamun. In another they are shown as if in a garden together. It is clear from the pictures that the couple ate together at meal times, enjoying roast duck, grapes, pomegranates and other fruit, and drinking wine or juices. Wine jars were found in the tomb, still with the dates of the vintages, together with a vast range of foods; including breads, joints of meat, spices and flavourings, fruits and two jars of honey for sweetening.

An 18th-dynasty tomb painting showing bakers mixing and kneading dough and filling bread moulds.

A tomb painting of female musicians at a banquet. One is playing the double flute while the others are clapping their hands.

WAS THEIR LIFE TOGETHER A HAPPY ONE?

It would seem so from the objects found in the tomb. Inside it there were flutes and harps and even a trumpet which could still be played. There were 4 complete board games too, and a ball. Tutankhamun's life was short, but it was mostly happy. However, the bodies of two tiny babies were also found in the tomb. They must have belonged to the royal couple, but they died before they were born. Tutankhamun had no heirs.

THE BUSINESS OF KINGSHIP

Egyptian society is often compared to a pyramid, with the king at the top, the officials in the middle and the peasants at the bottom. Tutankhamun would have had very little to do with the day-to-day running of Egypt. This was carried out by a vast number of officials. At the top of the civil service or government were the 2 viziers of Upper and Lower Egypt, the 2 administrative areas into which Egypt was divided. The vizier was the king's closest advisor, responsible for overseeing the collection of taxes. He was also the chief judge and the head of the civil service.

Everything in ancient Egypt was thought to belong to either the king or one of the gods, so everything had to be accounted for. This was done by a vast number of scribes working for the government or the many temples.

WHO WERE THESE EGYPTIAN SCRIBES?

With the exception of a number of key advisors and friends, very little is known about how Egypt was governed at the time of Tutankhamun. Most of the time, the king held meetings with his advisors. When something was decided, Tutankhamun would sign the necessary documents. Sometimes he would go on tours of Egypt, visiting the main towns and temples. However, where his father Akhenaten had been strong, Tutankhamun was weak.

Tutankhamun visits a town with his officials. He would have had little to do with the day-to-day running of Egypt but royal visits were always useful.

WHO REALLY RULED EGYPT?

For most of his reign Tutankhamun was a vulnerable little boy, controlled by his 2 powerful officials, Ay, the Chief Priest, and Horemheb, the commander of the army. Much of the day-to-day running of Egypt was performed by the priests in the temples and the scribes in the various government departments.

Maya, Tutankhamun's Minister of Finance and the Royal Scribe, was his friend.

Scribes checking accounts. Scribes were usually the sons of scribes. They were the 'managers' of Egypt, who gave orders, checked results, took records and granted or withheld permission.

DID TUTANKHAMUN TRUST AY AND HOREMHEB?

It is quite likely that he did not trust them, but he had no choice, because they were so powerful. Horemheb was even made deputy king, so that he could lead the army into Syria. Some historians think that Tutankhamun, as he grew older, started to demand more power for himself, and take an interest in government affairs.

Nahtmin had been Tutankhamun's tutor. There were 5 large wooden servant figures, 'shabtis', presented by him found in the tomb.

DID HE HAVE ANY FRIENDS?

Yes. We know that Tutankhamun did have one friend called Maya, who was his finance minister and the Royal Scribe. He also had the Queen, Ankhesenamun, to whom he was devoted, so he was not completely alone. Then there was also his tutor, the military officer, Nakhtmin, who may have been a relative of the king's grandmother, Queen Tiye.

DEATH OF A KING

No one knows exactly how Tutankhamun died. It may have been on a hunting trip that he met with an accident. His mummy showed a bruise on his face, which suggests he fell, perhaps from his chariot. Some historians think that Ay, or Horemheb, had Tutankhamun murdered, because he had started to demand more power for himself. But we cannot be sure of this, since we do not know what really happened. Tutankhamun was still only in his teens when he died.

This simple wooden statuette was left in Tutankhamun's tomb by Maya, his Minister of Finance. It shows the king as a mummy lying on a funeral bed inside a coffin, flanked by the soul of the dead king in the form of a bird.

We know that other members of Tutankhamun's family had been physically frail and died young. His brother Smenkhkare was probably only in his early twenties when he died.

Tutankhamun lies dead.

WHO RULED EGYPT AFTER HIS DEATH?

The general, Horemheb, was away in Syria with his army, fighting a people there called the Hittites. This gave Ay the chance to make himself king. Ay left a picture of himself in Tutankhamun's tomb. As Tutankhamun had no male heir, it was he who carried out the young king's funeral and arranged for all his treasure to be buried with him.

WHAT REACTION WAS THERE TO HIS DEATH?

Ay was probably glad. But Maya, the Finance Minister and Tutankhamun's friend, missed his young master. He left in the tomb a beautiful statuette. It showed Tutankhamun's soul in the form of a bird, looking at the body of the dead man, as if he could bring him to life again. His tutor, Nakhtmin, left 5 little servant statues in his tomb.

One of Nakhtmin's statues bore the inscription 'the servant who makes his master's name live'. The act of reviving the name of the dead during the burial ceremony was the duty of the eldest son. Since Tutankhamun died childless this would have been done by his closest relative or his most faithful friend.

A shabti figure in the form of Tutankhamun carrying agricultural tools. With the boy-king were buried a staggering 413 shabtis. Most private burials of the period were provided with one or perhaps two shabti figures.

DID ANYONE ELSE MOURN HIM?

Yes. We know that his young widow, Ankhesenamun, left a wreath of flowers on the top of the king's sarcophagus. They were flowers called persea, which only bloom in the spring, in the month of April – which is how we know that he died in April. They were still there when Howard Carter found them, 33 centuries later.

PREPARATIONS FOR IMMORTALITY

When the pharaoh's death was announced the whole country would have entered into a period of mourning. During this time all rejoicing was forbidden. The workshops of the craftsmen responsible for the tomb would have been frantically busy. They had to prepare the burial objects required for the different stages of the young king's journey to the next life. Everything had to be ready by the date of the funeral.

Tomb painting depicting carpenters and painters finishing two coffins.

WHAT HAPPENED TO HIS BODY?

For 70 days the embalmers would have worked on mummifying Tutankhamun's body. It had to last for eternity, so that the young king's soul could join his father, the sun-god, and watch over Egypt.

MUMMIFICATION

The king's internal organs, the lungs, liver and intestines were removed from his body, as well as his brain. His body was then wrapped in natron for about 70 days. Once it had de-hydrated, it was washed and anointed with spices. Finally came the bandaging, the last stage of embalming.

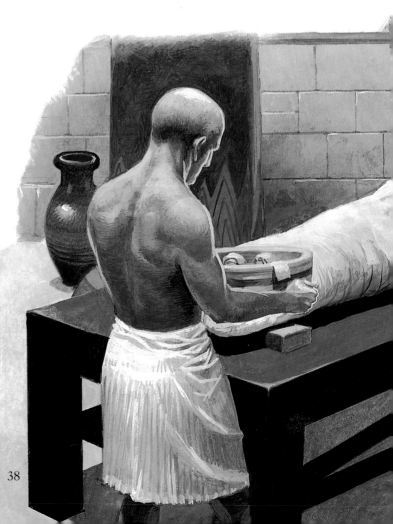

The king's body is coated with perfumed oils and resin, and wrapped in protective layers of linen bandages.

WAS THERE ANYTHING UNUSUAL ABOUT HIS BURIAL?

From what we know about the way the Egyptians buried their kings, Tutankhamun's burial was different. According to one Egyptologist it was 'fast and careless, within a hastily adapted private tomb, the corpse equipped with a ragbag mix of whatever new, old and adaptable funerary equipment was readily to hand'. Why this was no one knows. It may have been because work on Tutankhamun's intended place of burial had hardly begun.

A head of the sacred cow goddess, Hathor. Hathor was the goddess of the area where the tomb was found.

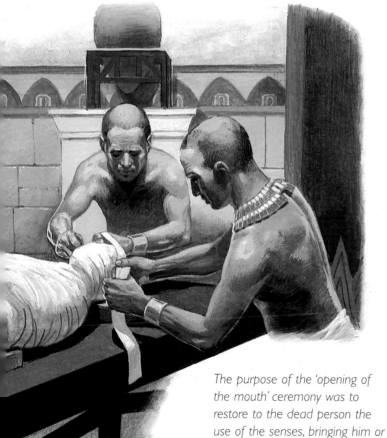

WHAT DO WE KNOW ABOUT HIS FUNERAL?

The funeral procession, followed by the highest officials of the land and by crowds of wailing women, would have wound its way up the Valley. It would have stopped, as was the custom, at various set points. We know that before placing his body in the tomb, Ay performed the ritual 'opening of the mouth', the ceremony of restoring to the king's mummy the use of its senses.

The purpose of the 'opening of the mouth' ceremony was to restore to the dead person the use of the senses, bringing him or her to life. Here a priest wearing the mask of Anubis, the jackal-god of mummification, is offering the mummy a bowl of holy water.

AFTER TUTANKHAMUN

Tutankhamun's young widow Ankhesenamun did not trust Ay. In desperation she wrote to the king of the Hittites, Egypt's old enemy, asking for a prince whom she could marry. The prince came, but he died on the way to Egypt; perhaps he was murdered.

This detail from the golden shrine, shows Ankhesenamun. No one knows for sure what happened to her after the king's death. It is possible that Ay married her to strengthen his claim to the throne.

WHAT HAPPENED TO THE QUEEN?

We do not know. We know that Ay reigned as king, but only for 4 years. It may be that he married Ankhesenamun to strengthen his claim to the throne. A ring was found with the names of the two of them combined. When Ay died in about 1319 BC the way was at last clear for Tutankhamun's general, Horemheb, to realise his dream of becoming king. He saw himself as the restorer of traditional order. One of his first acts was to reform the laws and to wipe out corruption which had flourished under weak government. Maya, Tutankhamun's friend, became his Minister of Finance.

A tomb painting of the god Osiris in the tomb of Horemheb. After Horemheb's death there was no male heir to inherit the throne. It passed to another general, Ramesses. He was the founder of the 19th dynasty.

A defaced statue of Amun at Karnak, carved in the image of Tutankhamun and originally inscribed with his name. The monument was taken over by Horemheb.

WHY WAS SO LITTLE KNOWN ABOUT TUTANKHAMUN UNTIL RECENTLY?

After the accession of Horemheb to the throne, the Amarna pharaohs – as Akhenaten and his two sons are known – became more and more unpopular. Their monuments were steadily dismantled. Eventually the decision was made to wipe Akhenaten and his two sons, Smenkhkare and Tutankhamun, out of the records, as if they had never existed.

The gold mask of the god-king of Egypt. Behind it was probably the face of a powerless young boy whose ambitious courtiers ran Egypt for their own gain.

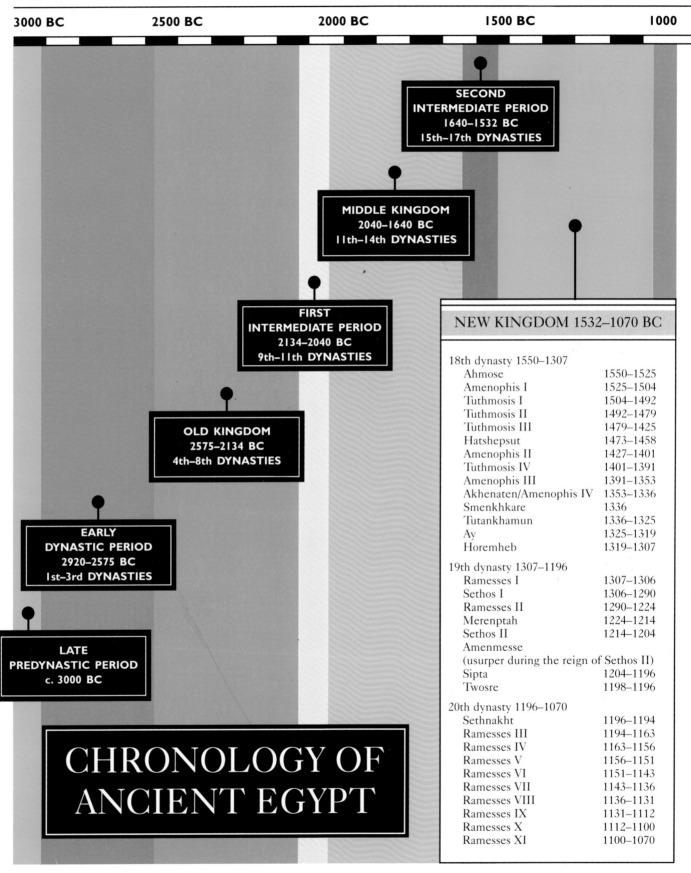

3000 BC	2500 BC	2000 BC	1500 BC	1000

SECOND INTERMEDIATE PERIOD
1640–1532 BC
15th–17th DYNASTIES

MIDDLE KINGDOM
2040–1640 BC
11th–14th DYNASTIES

FIRST INTERMEDIATE PERIOD
2134–2040 BC
9th–11th DYNASTIES

OLD KINGDOM
2575–2134 BC
4th–8th DYNASTIES

EARLY DYNASTIC PERIOD
2920–2575 BC
1st–3rd DYNASTIES

LATE PREDYNASTIC PERIOD
c. 3000 BC

CHRONOLOGY OF ANCIENT EGYPT

NEW KINGDOM 1532–1070 BC

18th dynasty 1550–1307
Ahmose	1550–1525
Amenophis I	1525–1504
Tuthmosis I	1504–1492
Tuthmosis II	1492–1479
Tuthmosis III	1479–1425
Hatshepsut	1473–1458
Amenophis II	1427–1401
Tuthmosis IV	1401–1391
Amenophis III	1391–1353
Akhenaten/Amenophis IV	1353–1336
Smenkhkare	1336
Tutankhamun	1336–1325
Ay	1325–1319
Horemheb	1319–1307

19th dynasty 1307–1196
Ramesses I	1307–1306
Sethos I	1306–1290
Ramesses II	1290–1224
Merenptah	1224–1214
Sethos II	1214–1204
Amenmesse	
(usurper during the reign of Sethos II)	
Sipta	1204–1196
Twosre	1198–1196

20th dynasty 1196–1070
Sethnakht	1196–1194
Ramesses III	1194–1163
Ramesses IV	1163–1156
Ramesses V	1156–1151
Ramesses VI	1151–1143
Ramesses VII	1143–1136
Ramesses VIII	1136–1131
Ramesses IX	1131–1112
Ramesses X	1112–1100
Ramesses XI	1100–1070

1000 BC	500 BC	I AD	500 AD	1000 AD

**THIRD INTERMEDIATE PERIOD
1070–712 BC
21st–25th DYNASTIES**

**LATE PERIOD
712–332 BC
25th DYNASTY and
2nd PERSIAN PERIOD**

**GRAECO-ROMAN PERIOD
332 BC–AD 395
MACEDONIAN DYNASTY
ROMAN EMPERORS**

TUTANKHAMUN'S FAMILY TREE

Tutankhamun was probably the son of Akhenaten, the son of Amenophis III and Tiye. His mother is likely to have been Kiya, a lesser wife of Akhenaten. Nefertiti and Akhenaten had six daughters, one of whom was later to become Tutankhamun's queen.

Amenophis III = *Tiye*

Kiya = *Akhenaten* = *Nefertiti*

Tutankhamun = *Ankhesenamun*
(3rd daughter)

43

GLOSSARY

AFTERLIFE The ancient Egyptians believed in life after death in a beautiful land that was like Egypt, but even better. But to get there the soul of the dead person had first to brave the perils of an underworld below the earth. The magic spells and HIEROGLYPHS on Tutankhamun's tomb were put there to protect against the dangers of this next world. If he could recite the correct spells the king could pass through unharmed and enter paradise, which the Egyptians called the Duat.

ANUBIS The jackal-headed god of the dead. He helped to prepare mummies and took the souls of the dead before Osiris, the stern judge of the underworld.

FUNERARY MODELS Some of the objects in the tomb were personal and had been used during the king's life. But others were made specially for his funeral to accompany him into the AFTERLIFE.

HIEROGLYPH A Greek word meaning 'sacred writing on stone'. It was used for official inscriptions on monuments. Some signs were pictures but some had a sound value as well as a pictorial one. There was also an alphabet of 24 consonants, as vowels were not written.

HORUS In ancient Egypt, the sky-god HORUS was believed to be the king's protector. He was portrayed as a falcon whose eyes were thought of as the sun and moon. In other forms HORUS was believed to ward off evil spirits.

KA A person's double who stayed with them after death. It was the KA who received the offerings of food and drink in the tomb.

NATRON Salt crystals found in the Egyptian desert and used in embalming.

NEKHABET The fierce vulture-goddess who protected the king. He wore the emblem of this goddess on his forehead.

OPET The chief festival in the Egyptian year. It took place on the Nile in October.

PHARAOH Title of the ruler of Egypt. The word means 'Great House' in Egyptian.

RA The sun-god and supposed ancestor of all the pharaohs. According to legend, he was born as a child every morning and died at night as an old man. He was usually shown with the head of a falcon topped with a sun disc, surrounded by the 'uraeus', the sacred flame-spitting cobra.

SCARAB BEETLE A type of beetle used to represent the Egyptian sun god.

SENET A board game symbolising the struggle against the forces of evil. There were 30 squares on the board and 2 sets of counters. The aim was to get all your pieces off the board and to stop your opponent doing the same. Moves were made according to the way the throwsticks (sticks rounded on one side and flat on the other) landed.

SHABTI A figure of the dead person placed with the body in the tomb to substitute for the dead person in any work required in the AFTERLIFE.

UPPER AND LOWER EGYPT The Egyptians saw their country in 2 parts: Upper Egypt, the river valley of the Nile to the south, and Lower Egypt, the delta marsh area to the north. The ruler of Egypt was called 'Lord of the Two Lands'. By the time of the New Kingdom, Upper and Lower Egypt were the 2 administrative areas of Egypt.

VALLEY OF THE KINGS For about 500 years from 1500 BC the pharaohs chose to be buried in a remote desert valley opposite the ancient city of Thebes on the River Nile in Upper Egypt. Their tombs were hidden deep in the cliffs where it was hoped robbers would not find them. Some of the queens and princes were buried in a nearby valley called the Valley of the Queens.

VIZIER The highest government official. By the New Kingdom there were 2 viziers – one of Lower Egypt based at Memphis in the north and one of Upper Egypt based at Thebes in the south.

INDEX

TUTANKHAMUN'S EGYPT AND THE VALLEY OF THE KINGS

WESTERN THEBES

VALLEY of the KINGS

West Valley

East Valley

Tomb of Amenophis III

Tomb of Ay

Tomb of Tiye

Tomb of Horemheb

TOMB OF TUTANKHAMUN

Tomb of Ramesses I

Temple of Hatsheput

Deir el-Bahri

Deir el-Medina

Valley of the Queens

Temple of Tuthmosis IV

site of Temple of Amenophis III

site of Palace of Amenophis III

Colossi of Memnon

Malqata

0   1 mile

0   2 km